CONTENTS

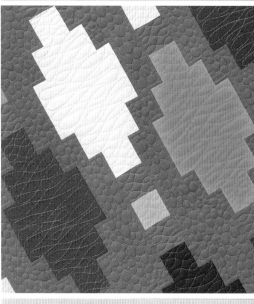

INTRODUCTION

Kona Cottons have been around for more than 30 years and in that time have become quite the staple for quilters who love working with solids. Interestingly enough, Robert Kaufman Fabrics introduced these solids that quilters have grown to love back in the mid 1980s, to go along with its line of Hawaiian prints. Those prints were used primarily for garments, as were most Robert Kaufman fabrics. But once quilters caught on to the 12 primary and bright colors being offered, it didn't take long until the line of colors was expanded.

What started as a dozen colors soon grew, and today there are a whopping 303 colors—from the most subtle of neutrals to extremely vivid brights and everything in between—giving today's quilters a range of choices like never before.

MAKE MINE KONA

In this collection of 13 fabulous quilts created by some of the brightest quilt designers around, you'll find that no two designers see color exactly the same way. And with 303 colors to choose from,

they don't have to! Some of the quilts in this book are quite modern, while others are a bit more traditional in design. Some are made with a very limited palette of just three colors, and others use 20 or more Kona hues. Seriously, could you limit yourself to just three colors when there are so many to choose from?

WE ASKED THE EXPERTS

To gain insight into why so many quilters love not only to design quilts for solid colors, but also why they choose Kona as their favorite solids, we asked each of the project designers in this book to share some of her thoughts on Kona Cotton solids. The designers named everthing from the weight to the weave to the bounty of beautiful colors. Take a look at what they had to say and see if you agree.

Debbie Grifka: I love the weight of Kona fabrics. And that there are so many great colors. And that my local quilt shop stocks the entire range. I'd use them even if my shop didn't carry them all, but that's a bonus for me!

Kristi Schroeder: I absolutely love the range of colors from the Kona Cotton line. I love the versatility of working with a neutral color palette. It appeals to a wide range of people and can go with any interior scheme.

Angela Walters: I love that they really show off the quilting. The fabric is so easy to quilt on and results in such beautiful textures!

Shea Henderson: The variety of colors is incredible and the ability to source them at various shops is super handy. I love to find a great inspiration photo from a magazine, and then pull colors from it using the chips in my Kona Color Card.

Nydia Kehnle: Kona is fantastic to work with. I prefer the body of Kona Cotton over other quality solids. I find them easier to cut and sew because they're less shifty than lighter-weight fabrics. I also love that they have 303 amazing colors to choose from. I have never had an issue with color bleeding and I do not prewash.

Heather Jones: I love working with Kona Cotton solids because there are so many different colors available. With more than 300 different hues, I can create just about any color palette imaginable!

Julie Herman: I like the variety of the colors available, the weight and the hand of the fabric, how it washes, and the feel of it after it's washed.

MAKE YOURS UNIQUE

The designers' passion for working with such wonderful cotton solids is clear, and we invite you to experience the same enjoyment and thrill as you piece your next quilt from solids. Whether you follow along using the same colors as shown, or you choose to put your own color spin on your quilt, the patterns in this book are designed to work well in solids. You'll find designs stitched in neutrals, some that feature just a pop of color, and those that are full-on rainbow riots.

If you'd like to do make a quilt exactly as it's shown, we've made it easy for you by giving the Kona color name. (After all, when then are dozens of greens and blues, being specific is the only way to go.) However, if you'd like to mix things up and color your own way, we've provided a little color reference for each quilt at the back of the book. That way, if you're not sure exactly what shade "frappe" or "mimosa" is, you can look it up on pages 62 and 63. All that makes color substitution easier, if that's your desire.

The Midnight Oasis bundle offers just the right amount of calm, with soothing blue-greens that range from pretty pastels to rich nighttime hues.

SPECTRUM

Designed and pieced by Julie Herman; quilted by Angela Walters

Aptly named, Spectrum's blocks range from the palest yellow to the darkest pink with assorted shades in between. The rainbow effect is accomplished with rows of easy blocks, each block consisting of only five pieces.

FINISHED QUILT: 60½" × 72½" • FINISHED BLOCK: 12" × 12"

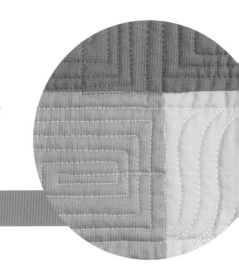

MATERIALS

Yardage is based on 42"-wide Kona Cotton solids except as noted. Fat quarters are 18" × 21".

30 fat quarters, 1 *each* of the following colors:

- Yellows: Yarrow, Grellow, Canary, Banana, Meringue
- Yellow-greens: Peridot, Bonsai, Peapod, Limelight, Wasabi
- Blue-greens: Celestial, Caribbean, Jade Green, Candy Green, Capri
- Blue-violets: Bright Periwinkle, Heliotrope, Morning Glory, Violet, Pansy
- Red-violets: Berry, Dark Violet, Geranium, Gumdrop, Blush Pink
- Pinks: Cerise, Valentine, Honeysuckle, Camellia, Bubble Gum

⅝ yard of Gumdrop for binding

4 yards of fabric for backing

69" × 81" piece of batting

CUTTING

Refer to the cutting diagrams below to make the best use of your fabric. All measurements include ¼"-wide seam allowances.

From the *2 darkest colors* in each group (12 total), cut:
5 rectangles, 4½" × 12½" (60 total)

From the *3 lightest colors* in each group (18 total), cut:
5 squares, 4½" × 4½" (90 total)

From the Gumdrop, cut:
7 strips, 2½" × 42"

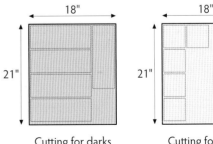

Cutting for darks   Cutting for lights

MAKING THE BLOCKS

Julie recommends pressing all seam allowances open as you construct your quilt.

1 Sew three yellow 4½" squares together in color-value order from lightest to medium to make a yellow 4½" × 12½" three-patch strip. Press. Make five strips.

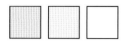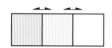

Make 5 strips,
4½" × 12½".

THREAD MATCHING

Julie recommends using a matching thread for each monochromatic row to piece the units, blocks, and rows. She chose Aurifil thread in the following colors: Yellow 5001, Green 1231, Blue 4182, Violet 2520, Berry 5003, and Pink 2530.

2 Join medium and dark yellow 4½" × 12½" rectangles to make a pieced 8½" × 12½" rectangle. Press. Make five pieced rectangles.

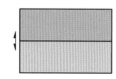

Make 5 units,
8½" × 12½".

3 Sew a yellow three-patch strip, with the darkest solid to the left, to the *bottom* of a pieced rectangle to make one block A, 12½" square, including the seam allowances. Make three.

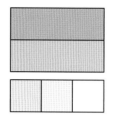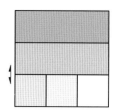

Block A.
Make 3 blocks, 12½" × 12½".

4 Sew a yellow three-patch strip, with the darkest solid to the left, to the *top* of a yellow rectangle to make one block B that's 12½" square. Make two.

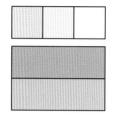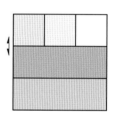

Block B.
Make 2 blocks, 12½" × 12½".

5 Referring to the quilt assembly diagram on page 9, join the blocks, alternating A and B, to make one yellow row, 12½" × 60½". Press.

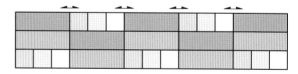

6 Repeat steps 1–5 with each color group to make six block rows. Press.

ASSEMBLING THE QUILT TOP

1 Lay out the rows in this order: yellow, yellow-green, blue-green, blue-violet, red-violet, and pink.

2 Sew the rows together. Press the seam allowances open to make a 60½" × 72½" quilt top.

FINISHING THE QUILT

For details on the following steps, download free information at ShopMartingale.com/HowtoQuilt.

1. Cut the backing into two 2-yard lengths. Sew the pieces together side by side.

2. Layer and baste the backing, batting, and quilt top. Quilt as desired. The quilt shown is quilted with ribbon, ribbon candy, swirl, and concentric rectangle designs.

3. Use the Gumdrop 2½"-wide strips to make double-fold binding, and then attach the binding to the quilt.

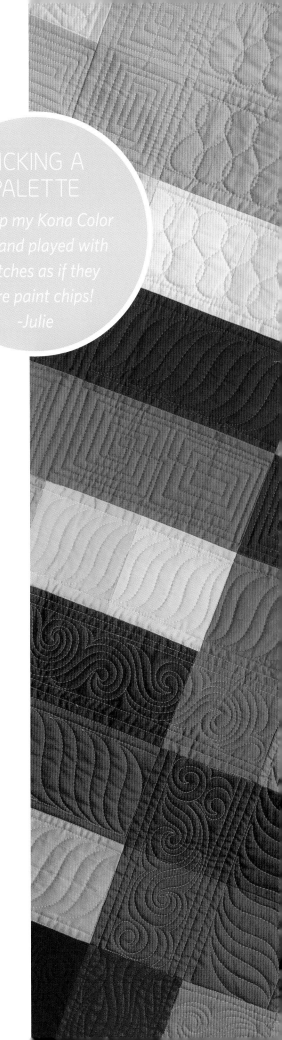

PICKING A PALETTE
I cut up my Kona Color Card and played with swatches as if they were paint chips!
-Julie

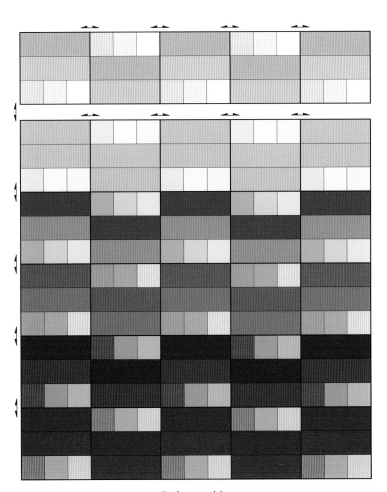

Quilt assembly

RAGGED EDGES

By Kristi Schroeder of Initial K Studio; quilted by Melissa Eubanks

This dramatic quilt is made almost entirely of half-square-triangle units. It's a project you can tackle in a weekend of easy, stress-free sewing.

FINISHED QUILT: 60½" × 70½"

MATERIALS

Yardage is based on 42"-wide Kona Cotton solids.

1¾ yards of Silver (A) for background

¾ yard *each* of Iron (B), Titanium (C), White (D), and Graphite (E) for half-square-triangle units

1 yard of Pepper (F) for half-square-triangle units and binding

4 yards of fabric for backing

69" × 79" piece of batting

CUTTING

All measurements include ¼"-wide seam allowances.

From the Silver, cut on the *lengthwise* grain:
2 strips, 8" × 60½"

From the remaining Silver, cut:
12 squares, 6" × 6"
6 rectangles, 5½" × 10½"

From the Iron, cut:
24 squares, 6" × 6"

From the Titanium, cut:
24 squares, 6" × 6"

From the White, cut:
24 squares, 6" × 6"

From the Graphite, cut:
24 squares, 6" × 6"

From the Pepper, cut:
12 squares, 6" × 6"
7 strips, 2½" × 42"

MAKING THE HALF-SQUARE-TRIANGLE UNITS

Press all seam allowances as shown by the arrows in the illustrations.

1 Draw a diagonal line from corner to corner on the wrong side of the Silver squares and 12 *each* of the Iron, Titanium, White, and Graphite squares.

2 Place one Silver square on one unmarked Iron square, right sides together. Sew ¼" away from the drawn line on both sides. Cut on the drawn line to make two half-square-triangle units. Trim the units to measure 5½" square. Press.

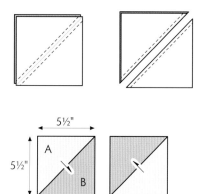

3 Repeat step 2 to make 24 half-square-triangle units in each color combination as shown. Trim each unit to measure 5½" square.

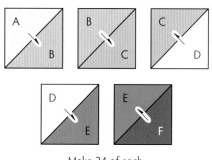

Make 24 of each,
5½" × 5½".

PLAYING FAVORITES

Titanium is a great neutral that goes with a wide range of colors.
-Kristi

ASSEMBLING THE QUILT TOP

1 Referring to the quilt assembly diagram below, lay out the half-square-triangle units and Silver rectangles in 11 horizontal rows.

2 Sew the units together in each row. Press.

3 Sew the rows together. Press.

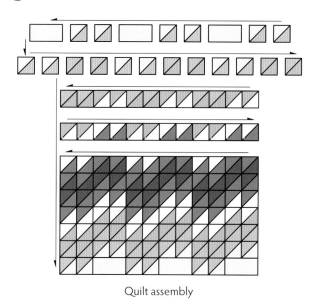

Quilt assembly

4 Sew the Silver 8" × 60½" strips to the top and bottom. Press. The quilt top should measure 60½" × 70½".

FINISHING THE QUILT

For details on the following steps, download free information at ShopMartingale.com/HowtoQuilt.

1 Cut the backing into two 2-yard lengths. Sew the pieces together lengthwise.

2 Layer and baste the backing, batting, and quilt top. Quilt as desired. The quilt shown is quilted in straight lines echoing the diagonal shapes.

3 Use the Pepper 2½"-wide strips to make double-fold binding, and then attach the binding to the quilt.

LANTERNS

Designed and made by Christa Watson

Using a precut bundle is a great way to make an all-solid quilt. The colors have been carefully coordinated, so you know they'll look great together. Choose a Roll Up of your favorite colors along with a neutral color such as the Coal used here to create this dynamic modern design.

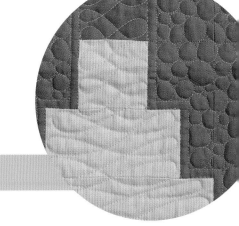

FINISHED QUILT: 60½" × 72½" • FINISHED BLOCK: 6" × 12" and 6" × 6"

MATERIALS

Yardage is based on 42"-wide Kona Cotton solids. See "Solid Advice from Christa" on page 17 for specifics about the colors she used.

40 bright precut strips, 2½" × 42" (or 1 Roll Up) for blocks (assorted red, orange, yellow, and green solids)*

3¼ yards of Coal for background and binding

4 yards of fabric for backing

69" × 81" piece of batting

*If using yardage, select assorted red, orange, yellow, and green solids to total ¾ to 1 yard of each color.

CUTTING

All measurements include ¼"-wide seam allowances.

From *each* 2½" × 42" bright strip, cut:
2 rectangles, 2½" × 6½"
2 rectangles, 2½" × 4½"
3 squares, 2½" × 2½"

From the Coal, cut:
43 strips, 2½" × 42" ; crosscut:
    14 strips into 80 rectangles, 2½" × 6½"
    15 strips into 240 squares, 2½" × 2½"
    7 strips into 160 rectangles, 1½" × 2½"
The 7 remaining strips are for binding.

STAY ORGANIZED

Keep like fabrics together, and set aside one of the squares for the smaller blocks. For faster cutting, fold the strips and stack two strips so you're cutting through four layers at once.

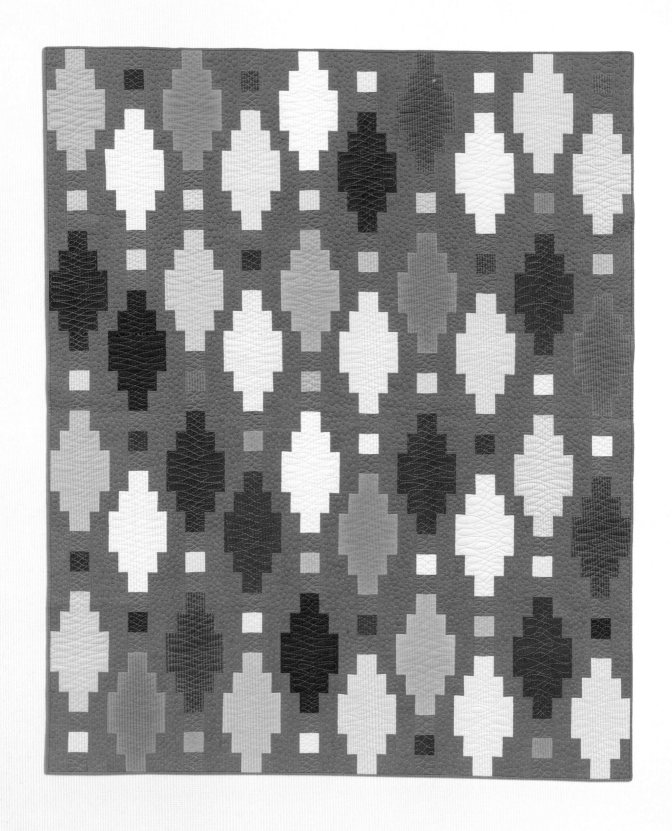

PIECING THE LANTERN BLOCKS

Press all seam allowances as shown by the arrows in the illustrations.

1 Lay out two Coal squares, two Coal 1½" × 2½" rectangles, one bright square, one bright 2½" × 4½" rectangle, and one bright 2½" × 6½" rectangle (all matching) in three rows as shown. Sew the units together in each row. Press.

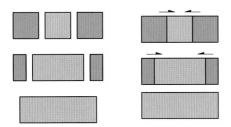

2 Join the rows to make a 6½" × 6½" half-lantern unit. Make two matching half-lantern units.

3 Sew the half-lantern units together to make a 6½" × 12½" Lantern block. Press. Make 40 Lantern blocks.

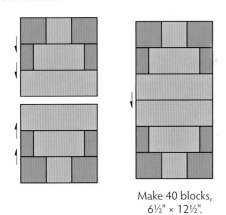

Make 40 blocks,
6½" × 12½".

PIECING THE SQUARE BLOCKS

1 Sew two Coal squares to opposite sides of a bright square. Press. Make 40.

Make 40 units,
2½" × 6½".

SPEEDY PIECING

For faster assembly, chain piece the units by sewing one pair together; then add the next pair under the presser foot without clipping threads between the pairs.

2 Sew two Coal 2½" × 6½" rectangles to the remaining sides of one unit to make a Square block that measures 6½" square, including the seam allowances. Press. Make 40 Square blocks.

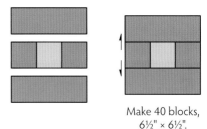

Make 40 blocks,
6½" × 6½".

ASSEMBLING THE QUILT TOP

1 Lay out the Lantern blocks, alternating them with the Square blocks, in 10 vertical rows as shown in the quilt assembly diagram on page 16. The odd-numbered rows will start with Lantern blocks and end with Square blocks; the even-numbered rows will be the opposite.

EASY ROW ASSEMBLY

Turn the Lantern blocks so that the center seam alternates direction from row to row for easy seam matching as you sew the blocks together.

2   Sew the blocks together in each row. Press.

3   Sew the rows together. Press. The quilt top
    should measure 60½" × 72½".

FINISHING THE QUILT

For details on the following steps, you can download
free information at ShopMartingale.com/HowtoQuilt.

1   Cut the backing into two 2-yard lengths. Sew the
    pieces together side by side.

2   Layer and baste the backing, batting, and quilt
    top. The quilt shown is quilted with a ribbon
design in the bright areas and an allover pebble
design in the background.

3   Use the Coal 2½"-wide strips to make double-
    fold binding, and then attach the binding to
the quilt.

MACHINE-QUILTING EXPERTISE

*For more machine-quilting suggestions, check
out Christa's books:* Machine Quilting with
Style *(Martingale, 2015) and* The Ultimate
Guide to Machine Quilting *(with Angela
Walters, Martingale, 2016).*

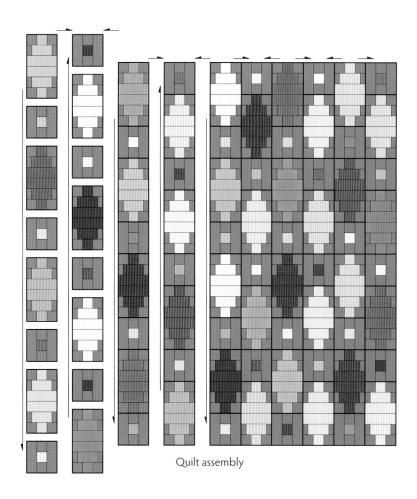

Quilt assembly

PICKING A
PALETTE

*I balanced the fiery palette
of this quilt by adding a
soothing splash of green
to cool it down a bit.*
-Christa

SOLID ADVICE FROM CHRISTA

When choosing colors to make this quilt, Christa used an analogous color scheme consisting of four colors that lie next to each other on the color wheel.

Christa chose a total of 28 reds, oranges, yellows, and greens, which collectively are known as the Christa Watson Designer Palette. Purchase this Roll Up at your favorite quilt shop or online from the Precut Store (available at ThePrecutStore.com). Colors included in this bundle are: Lime, Sprout, Peapod, Cactus, Zucchini, Artichoke, Curry, Corn Yellow, Sunflower, Buttercup, Canary, Citrus, Cheddar, Papaya, School Bus, Orange, Mango, Carrot, Tangerine, Flame, Coral, Lipstick, Tomato, Poppy, Red, Pomegranate, Ruby, and Rich Red.

Kona Coal is a perfect complement to this high-energy palette, creating a glowing effect when combined with the rich citrus colors.

Although this design would look great in prints, using solids allows the geometric shapes to stand out, creating defined edges between the blocks and the background.

Christa enjoys working with solids because they allow the quilting to shine, which is her favorite part of the quiltmaking process. Also, with solids, there's no worry about the orientation of directional prints or which is the right or wrong side of the fabric. This gives the quilter freedom to concentrate on creating more interesting designs, and the sewing seems to go a lot faster, too!

GANDER

Designed and pieced by Shea Henderson; quilted by Ruth Doss

Large Flying Geese blocks, going this way and that, give this quilt its appeal, and the use of both warm and cool colors adds bold contrast. The curves of the Baptist Fan quilting pattern perfectly complement the angular design.

FINISHED QUILT: 60½" × 72½"

MATERIALS

Yardage is based on 42"-wide Kona Cotton solids.

1 yard of Flame (A) for blocks

1 yard of Kumquat (B) for blocks

1 yard of Natural (C) for blocks

1⅞ yards of Aqua (D) for blocks and binding

1 yard of Azure (E) for blocks

4½ yards of fabric for backing

69" × 81" piece of batting

CUTTING

All measurements include ¼"-wide seam allowances.

From the Flame, cut:
5 squares, 13¼" × 13¼"
4 squares, 6⅞" × 6⅞"

From the Kumquat, cut:
1 square, 13¼" × 13¼"
16 squares, 6⅞" × 6⅞"

From the Natural, cut:
2 squares, 13¼" × 13¼"
12 squares, 6⅞" × 6⅞"

From the Aqua, cut:
3 squares, 13¼" × 13¼"
20 squares, 6⅞" × 6⅞"
7 strips, 2½" × 42"

From the Azure, cut:
4 squares, 13¼" × 13¼"
8 squares, 6⅞" × 6⅞"

MAKING THE FLYING GEESE BLOCKS

This quilt uses a time-saving construction method for making Flying Geese blocks. You'll make the geese four at a time; don't be alarmed if the cut sizes seem too large for the final block. Press all seam allowances as shown by the arrows in the illustrations.

1 Draw a diagonal line on the wrong side of each 6⅞" square.

2 Place two marked Aqua squares on opposite corners of one Flame 13¼" square, aligning the outer edges. (The squares will overlap slightly in the center of the large square.) Sew ¼" away from the diagonal line on both sides. Cut on the line to make two half-flying-geese units. Press.

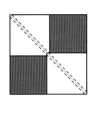 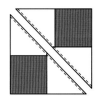

3 Place a marked Aqua square on the remaining corner of each half-flying-geese unit with the drawn line perpendicular to the seam. Sew ¼" away from the diagonal lines on both sides. Cut on the lines to make four 6½" × 12½" Aqua/Flame flying-geese units. Press.

4 Make a total of 60 flying-geese units in the amounts shown using the marked squares and 13¼" squares.

Make 8 units,
6½" × 12½".

Make 4 units,
6½" × 12½".

Make 8 units,
6½" × 12½".

Make 4 units,
6½" × 12½".

Make 4 units,
6½" × 12½".

Make 4 units,
6½" × 12½".

Make 8 units,
6½" × 12½".

Make 4 units,
6½" × 12½".

Make 4 units,
6½" × 12½".

Make 4 units,
6½" × 12½".

Make 8 units,
6½" × 12½".

5 Sew two matching flying-geese units together to make one 12½" square Flying Geese block. Press. Make 30 Flying Geese blocks.

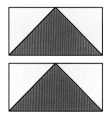 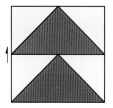

Make 30 blocks,
12½" × 12½".

ASSEMBLING THE QUILT TOP

1 Lay out the blocks in six rows of five blocks each as shown in the quilt assembly diagram on page 21, noting the orientation of each block. Sew the blocks together in each row. Press the seam allowances in opposite directions from row to row.

2 Sew the rows together. Press the seam allowances in one direction to complete a 60½" × 72½" quilt top.

Quilt assembly

FINISHING THE QUILT

For details on the following steps, download free information at ShopMartingale.com/HowtoQuilt.

1 Cut the backing into two 2¼-yard lengths. Sew the pieces together side by side.

2 Layer and baste the backing, batting, and quilt top. Quilt as desired. The quilt shown is machine quilted with a Baptist Fan design.

3 Use the Aqua 2½"-wide strips to make double-fold binding, and then attach the binding to the quilt.

PLAYING FAVORITES

Kona Bone is my favorite. I have used bolts of that color!
-Shea

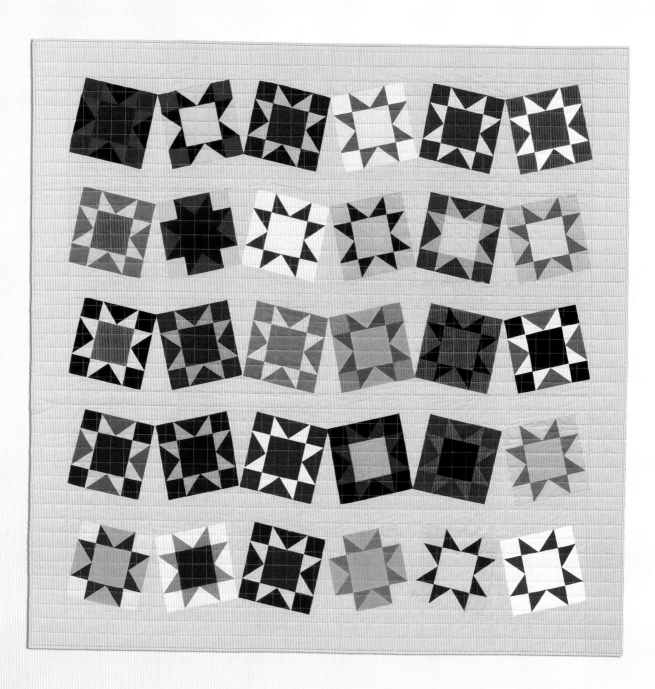

SOLOMON STARS

Designed and pieced by Anita Grossman Solomon

A whimsical tilted setting is just right for these colorful, scrappy Star blocks. Anita devised a technique for cutting simple square-on-point units and rearranging them to make the stars. Who could resist?

FINISHED QUILT: 65½" × 64" • FINISHED BLOCK: 9½" × 9½"

MATERIALS

Yardage is based on 42"-wide Kona Cotton solids.

3½ yards of Parchment for background, borders, and binding

31 fat eighths, 1 *each* of the following colors: Aloe, Berry, Blue Jay, Bonsai, Cedar, Celestial, Charcoal, Coral, Cream, Crimson, Graphite, Grellow, Indigo, Lapis, Pepper, Pickle, Pomegranate, Raisin, Regatta, Ruby, Sangria, School Bus, Seafoam, Shadow, Shale, Slate, Snow, Tomato, Ultra Marine, Wasabi, and Yarrow*

4¼ yards of fabric for backing

73" × 72" piece of batting

Template plastic

*When cutting fat eighths for the Star blocks, Anita also cut a few pieces from leftover scraps of Parchment so that some shapes would appear to float against the background. She also used 31 fat eighths, even though there are only 30 blocks, for variety.

CUTTING

Using the template plastic and the pattern on page 26, make a triangle template. All measurements include ¼"-wide seam allowances.

From the Parchment, cut on the *lengthwise* grain:
2 strips, 4½" × 64"
2 strips, 4½" × 57½"
4 strips, 2½" × 57½"

From the remaining Parchment, cut on the *crosswise* grain:
7 strips, 2½" × 42"
60 triangles and 60 reversed triangles

From *each* of the fat eighths, cut:
1 square, 6⅞" × 6⅞" (31 total)
2 squares, 6" × 6"; cut both squares in half diagonally to yield 4 triangles (124 total)

MAKING THE STAR BLOCKS

Press all seam allowances as shown by the arrows in the illustrations.

1 Sew two matching triangles to opposite sides of a different-colored 6⅞" square. Press. Sew two matching triangles to the remaining sides of the square. Press. Trim the unit to 9½" square.

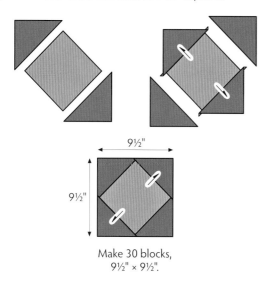

Make 30 blocks,
9½" × 9½".

2 Using a rotary cutter, cut each unit 2½" away from each edge without moving the pieces.

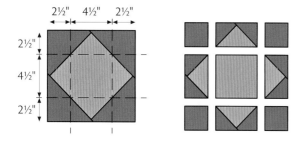

CUTTING THE BLOCKS

Use a revolving mat, or a small mat that you can turn, so that you can cut in all four directions without moving the fabric pieces.

3 Sort the pieces into 30 groups. Each group will include one center 4½" square, four matching flying-geese 2½" × 4½" units, and four matching corner 2½" squares. Choose combinations that are pleasing to you.

4 Using your selected pieces, sew two flying-geese units to opposite sides of one center square. Press. Sew a corner square to each end of the remaining flying-geese units. Press.

5 Sew the units together to make a Star block that's 8½" square, including the seam allowances. Make 30 Star blocks.

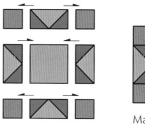
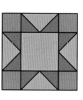

Make 30 blocks,
8½" × 8½".

FRAMING THE STAR BLOCKS

1 To make a Left Star block, sew one reversed frame triangle to the top of a Star block (the wide end should be to the left). Press the seam allowances toward the triangle. Working clockwise around the block, sew a reversed frame triangle to each remaining side of the Star block in the same manner to make a Left Star block that measures 10" square, including the seam allowances. Make 15.

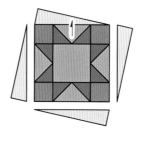
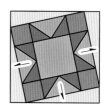

Left Star block.
Make 15 blocks, 10" × 10".

2 To make a Right Star block, sew a frame triangle to the top of a Star block (the wide end should be to the right). Press the seam allowances toward the triangle. Working counterclockwise, sew

a frame triangle to each remaining side of the Star block in the same manner to make a Right Star block that measures 10" square, including the seam allowances. Make 15.

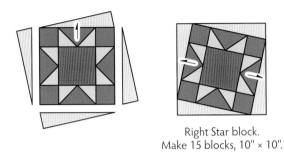

Right Star block.
Make 15 blocks, 10" × 10".

MANAGING THE POINTS

Use a fabric glue stick to hold the last triangle tip in place.

ASSEMBLING THE QUILT TOP

1 Lay out the blocks, alternating the Right Star and Left Star blocks, in five horizontal rows of six blocks each. Sew the blocks together in each row. Press.

2 Sew the block rows and the four Parchment 2½" × 57½" sashing strips together, alternating them to complete the quilt center, which should measure 57½" × 56". Press.

3 Sew the Parchment 4½" × 57½" strips to the top and bottom of the quilt center. Press the seam allowances toward the borders.

4 Sew the Parchment 4½" × 64" strips to the sides of the quilt center. Press the seam allowances toward the borders to complete a 65½" × 64" quilt top.

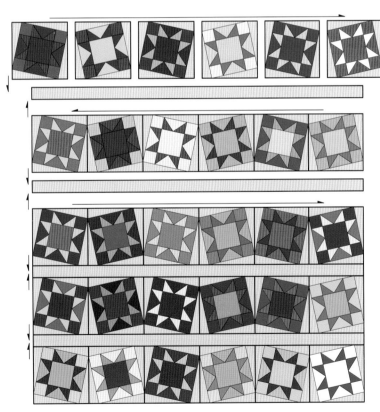

Quilt assembly

FINISHING THE QUILT TOP

For details on the following steps, download free information at ShopMartingale.com/HowtoQuilt.

1 Cut the backing fabric into 2⅛-yard lengths. Sew the pieces together lengthwise.

2 Layer and baste the backing, batting, and quilt top. Quilt as desired. The quilt shown is quilted in a grid of straight lines placed 1½" apart.

3 Use the Parchment 2½"-wide strips to make double-fold binding, and then attach the binding to the quilt.

MUST-HAVE

My favorite color is Bonsai. But I want to dance with Aloe, marry Indigo, and name my firstborn Grellow.
-Anita

¼" seam allowance

Frame triangle
Cut 15 sets of 4 matching and 15 reversed sets of 4 matching.

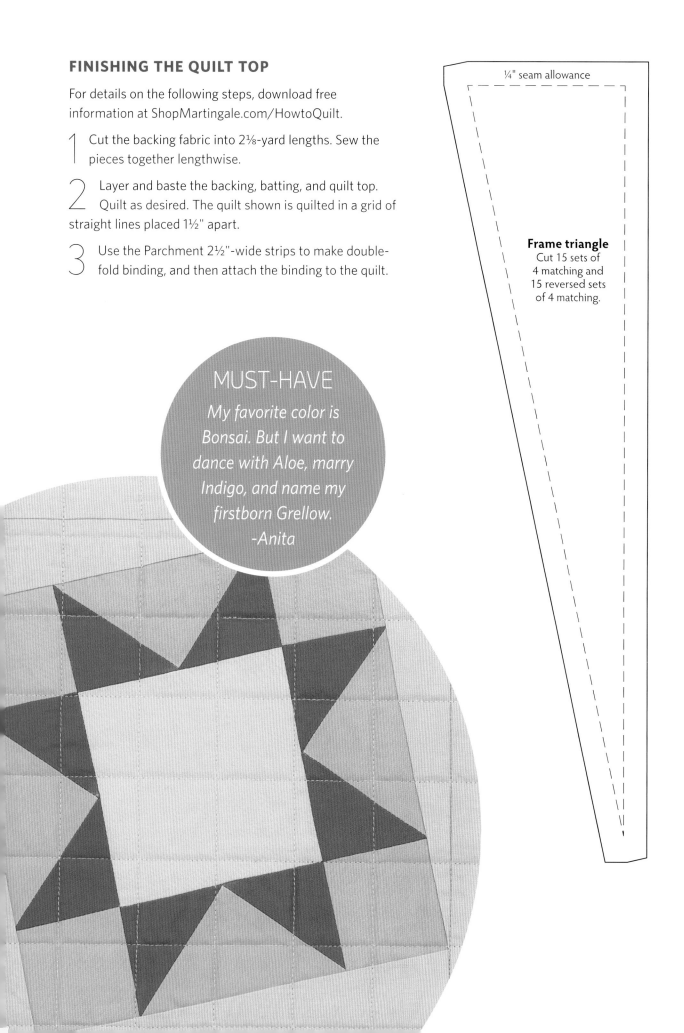

BIG COURTHOUSE SQUARE

Designed and pieced by Heather Jones

Less is more *describes this easy-to-piece throw. With just three colors and 21 pieces in the entire quilt, making it provides instant gratification. Take a break from long-term projects to make this bold Courthouse Steps quilt today!*

FINISHED QUILT: 66½" × 66½"

MATERIALS

Yardage is based on 42"-wide Kona Cotton solids.

2½ yards of Slate for strips

2 yards of Pearl Pink for strips

¾ yard of Mango for center square and binding

4¼ yards of fabric for backing

75" × 75" piece of batting

CUTTING

As you cut the fabric, keep all pieces organized by labeling each stack with masking tape marked with the appropriate letter. All measurements include ¼"-wide seam allowances.

From the Slate, cut:

1 panel, 66½" × 42"; cut into:
    2 strips, 6½" × 66½" (K)
    2 strips, 6½" × 54½" (I)
    2 strips, 6½" × 42½" (G)

3 strips, 6½" × 42"; crosscut into:
    2 strips, 6½" × 30½" (E)
    2 strips, 6½" × 18½" (C)

From the Pearl Pink, cut:

1 panel, 55" × 42"; cut into:
    2 strips, 6½" × 54½" (J)
    2 strips, 6½" × 30½" (F)
    2 strips, 6½" × 42½" (H)

2 strips, 6½" × 42"; crosscut into:
    2 strips, 6½" × 18½" (D)
    2 squares, 6½" × 6½" (B)

From the Mango, cut:

1 square, 6½" × 6½" (A)

7 strips, 2½" × 42"

SEWING LONG STRIPS

Fold each strip in half crosswise and mark the center on both edges. When adding each strip, pin the strip to the center section at both ends and at the marks. Sew with the strip on top, aligning the edges as you sew.

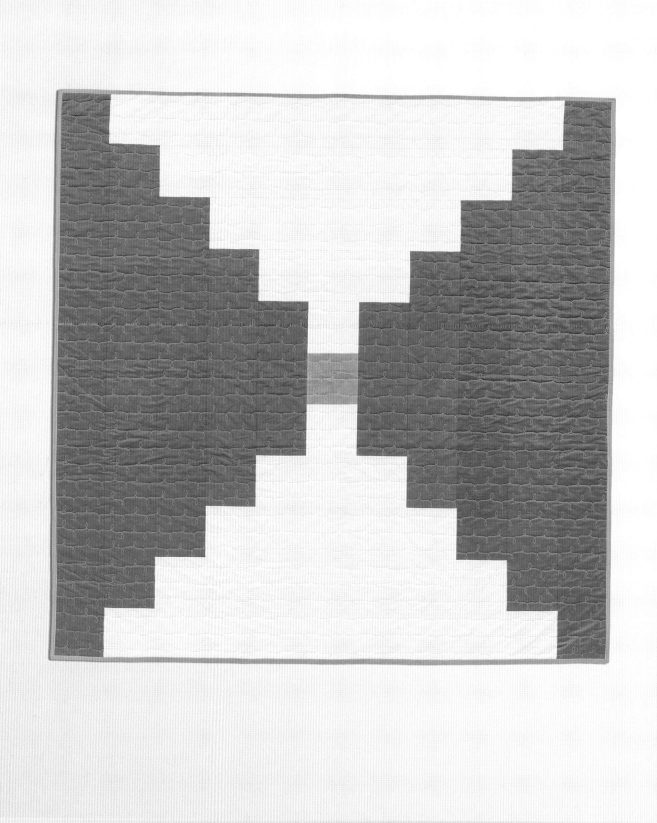

ASSEMBLING THE QUILT TOP

Press each seam allowance toward the last strip added, as indicated by the arrows.

1 Sew the Pearl Pink B squares to the top and bottom of the Mango A square to make a three-patch unit. Press.

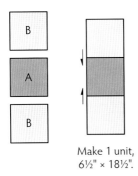

Make 1 unit,
6½" × 18½".

2 Sew the Slate C strips to the three-patch unit to make the center square. Press.

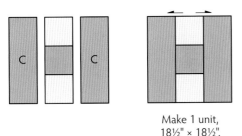

Make 1 unit,
18½" × 18½".

3 Continue adding the strips in alphabetical order to complete a 66½" square quilt top.

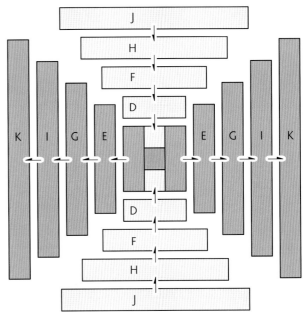

Quilt assembly

FINISHING THE QUILT

For details on the following steps, download free information at ShopMartingale.com/HowtoQuilt.

1 Cut the backing into two 2⅛-yard lengths. Sew the pieces together side by side.

2 Layer and baste the backing, batting, and quilt top. Quilt as desired. The quilt shown is machine quilted in a 2" grid of lines with little loops.

3 Use the Mango 2½"-wide strips to make double-fold binding, and then attach the binding to the quilt.

PICKING A PALETTE

I love the combination of Slate and Pearl Pink with a pop of Mango.
-Heather

MOSAIC GEMS

Designed and pieced by Cortney Heimerl

The Trip around the World design has been made countless times, but this modern version is unique because it's laid out in colorful columns rather than as a grid of blocks. That difference gives the quilt a mosaic appearance.

FINISHED QUILT: 54½" × 66½"

MATERIALS

Yardage is based on 42"-wide Kona Cotton solids.

¼ yard of Nightfall for squares

¼ yard of Grapemist for squares

⅜ yard of Nectarine for squares

¼ yard of Honeysuckle for squares

½ yard of Natural for squares

⅔ yard of Baby Blue for squares

¼ yard of Creamsicle for squares

¾ yard of Buttercup for squares

½ yard of Pewter for squares

⅞ yard of Lilac for squares

¾ yard of Lagoon for squares

1 yard of Evergreen for squares and binding

3½ yards of fabric for backing

63" × 75" piece of batting

CUTTING

All measurements include ¼"-wide seam allowances.

From the Nightfall, cut:
32 squares, 2½" × 2½"

From the Grapemist, cut:
16 squares, 2½" × 2½"

From the Nectarine, cut:
56 squares, 2½" × 2½"

From the Honeysuckle, cut:
16 squares, 2½" × 2½"

From the Natural, cut:
68 squares, 2½" × 2½"

From the Baby Blue, cut:
116 squares, 2½" × 2½"

From the Creamsicle, cut:
46 squares, 2½" × 2½"

From the Buttercup, cut:
129 squares, 2½" × 2½"

From the Pewter, cut:
66 squares, 2½" × 2½"

From the Lilac, cut:
148 squares, 2½" × 2½"

From the Lagoon, cut:
130 squares, 2½" × 2½"

From the Evergreen, cut:
68 squares, 2½" × 2½"
7 strips, 2½" × 42"

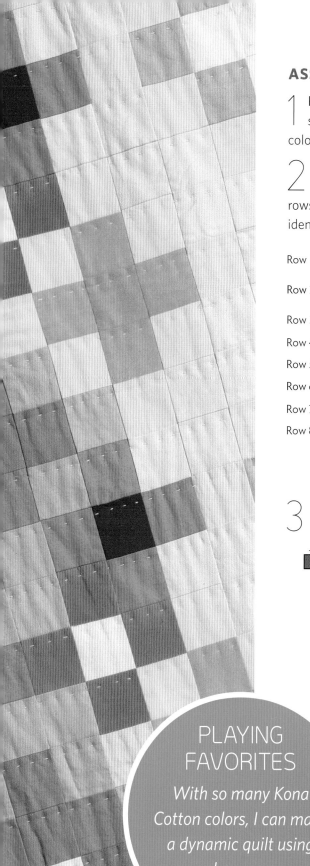

ASSEMBLING THE QUILT SECTIONS

1 Referring to the quilt assembly diagram on page 33, lay out the squares in eight rows of 27 squares each, paying careful attention to color placement.

2 Sew the squares together in each row. Press the seam allowances in rows 1, 3, 5, and 7 to the right and press the seam allowances in rows 2, 4, 6, and 8 to the left to make a 16½" × 54½" section. Make four identical sections.

Row 1
Row 2
Row 3
Row 4
Row 5
Row 6
Row 7
Row 8

Make 4 units,
16½" × 54½".

3 Sew the 27 remaining 2½" squares together as shown to make the bottom row. Press the seam allowances to the right.

Make 1 bottom row,
2½" × 54½".

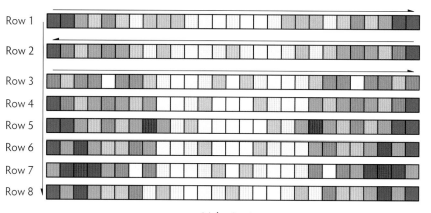

CHAIN SEW

Make the four large sections at the same time by chain sewing units that are the same. For example: Join the first two squares, chain sewing four matching pairs. Continue chain sewing squares in four matching pairs. Separate the pairs into four groups as you cut them apart.

PLAYING FAVORITES

With so many Kona Cotton colors, I can make a dynamic quilt using only squares.
-Cortney

ASSEMBLING THE QUILT TOP

1 Sew the four quilt sections together.

2 Add the bottom row to complete a 54½" × 66½" quilt top. Press the seam allowances in one direction.

FINISHING THE QUILT

For details on the following steps, download free information at ShopMartingale.com/HowtoQuilt.

1 Cut the backing into two 1¾-yard lengths. Sew the pieces together side by side.

2 Layer and baste the backing, batting, and quilt top. Quilt as desired. The quilt shown is hand quilted ¼" away from each horizontal seam.

3 Use the Evergreen 2½"-wide strips to make double-fold binding, and then attach the binding to the quilt.

Quilt assembly

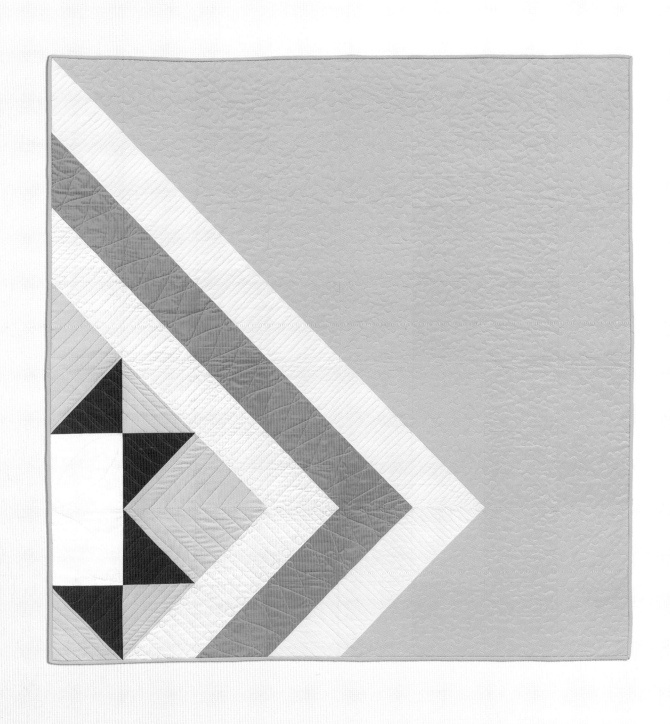

ZOOMER

Designed and pieced by Elizabeth Dackson

An asymmetrical design unites with cool blue solids for one "cool" quilt! Using a quick half-square-triangle technique makes assembly easy for quilters of all skill levels.

FINISHED QUILT: 64½" × 64½"

MATERIALS

Yardage is based on 42"-wide Kona Cotton solids.

1 fat quarter of Ice Frappe for patchwork

⅝ yard of Niagara for patchwork

1 fat quarter of Celestial for patchwork

⅝ yard of Baby Blue for patchwork

⅝ yard of Oasis for patchwork

⅝ yard of Pond for patchwork

3½ yards of Candy Green for patchwork and binding

4¼ yards of fabric for backing

73" × 73" piece of batting

CUTTING

All measurements include ¼"-wide seam allowances.

From the Ice Frappe, cut:
2 squares, 8½" × 8½"

From the Niagara, cut:
2 squares, 17¾" × 17¾"

From the Celestial, cut:
1 square, 17¾" × 17¾"

From the Baby Blue, cut:
2 squares, 17¾" × 17¾"

From the Oasis, cut:
2 squares, 17¾" × 17¾"

From the Pond, cut:
2 squares, 17¾" × 17¾"

From the Candy Green, cut:
1 panel, 57" × 42"; cut into:
    1 strip, 8½" × 56½" (A)
    1 strip, 8½" × 48½" (B)
    1 strip, 8½" × 40½" (C)
    1 strip, 8½" × 32½" (D)
1 panel, 25" × 42"; cut into:
    2 strips, 8½" × 24½" (E)
    2 strips, 8½" × 16½" (F)
1 square, 17¾" × 17¾"
7 strips, 2½" × 42"

MAKING THE
HALF-SQUARE-TRIANGLE UNITS

Press all seam allowances as shown by the arrows in the illustrations.

1 Draw a diagonal line from corner to corner in each direction on the wrong side of each Niagra, Oasis, and Candy Green 17¾" square.

2 Place a Celestial square on a Niagara square, right sides together. Sew ¼" from both sides of each drawn line.

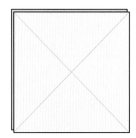 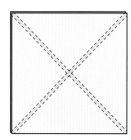

3 Cut the sewn unit into quarters through the middle, lengthwise and widthwise. Then cut on each of the marked lines to make eight half-square-triangle units that measure 8½" square. (Four units will be extra.) Press the seam allowances open.

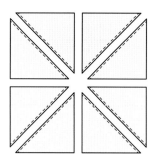

Make 8 units,
8½" × 8½".

4 In the same manner, make eight *each* of Niagra/Baby Blue, Baby Blue/Oasis, Oasis/Pond, and Pond/Candy Green half-square-triangle units. You will have some leftover units.

Make 8 of each.

ASSEMBLING THE QUILT

1 Lay out the half-square-triangle units, Ice Frappe squares, and Candy Green rectangles A–F in eight rows as shown in the quilt assembly diagram below. Set aside the remaining half-square-triangle units to sew into the backing, if desired.

2 Sew the squares and rectangles together in each row. Press.

3 Sew the rows together to complete a 64½"-square quilt top. Press.

FINISHING THE QUILT

For details on the following steps, download free information at ShopMartingale.com/HowtoQuilt.

1 Cut the backing fabric into two 2⅛-yard lengths. Sew the pieces together side by side.

2 Layer and baste the backing, batting, and quilt top. Quilt as desired. The quilt shown is machine quilted with straight lines in the star section, serpentine lines in the strips, and meandering in the background.

3 Use the Candy Green 2½"-wide strips to make double-fold binding, and then attach the binding to the quilt.

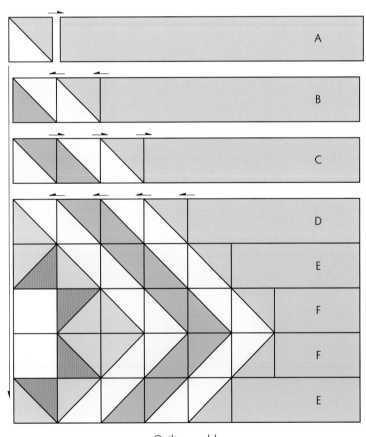

Quilt assembly

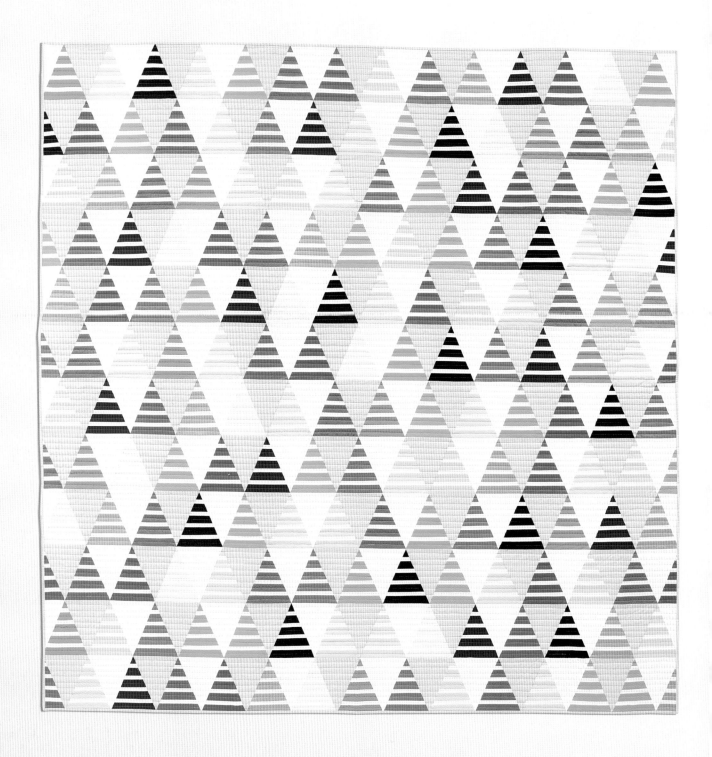

A NEW DAY

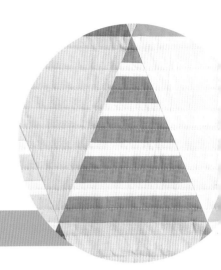

Designed and pieced by Megan Pitz

The triangles in this quilt only look like they're cut from striped fabrics. You'll make strip sets and then cut triangles from them. A splash of yellow among the various blues and greens interrupts the hard lines and adds pizzazz.

FINISHED QUILT: 98½" × 84½"

MATERIALS

Yardage is based on 42"-wide Kona Cotton solids.

⅝ yard *each* of 14 yellow, blue, and green solids: Wasabi, Cactus, Chartreuse, Lime, Kiwi, Clover, Kale, Cypress, Bahama Blue, Lagoon, Oasis, Deep Blue, Regal, and Amethyst

5¾ yards of White for background

3⅛ yards of Shadow for background and binding

7⅞ yards of fabric for backing

106" × 92" piece of batting

Template plastic

CUTTING

All measurements include ¼"-wide seam allowances.

From *each* of the yellow, blue, and green solids, cut:
4 strips, 1¾" × 42" (56 total)
6 strips, 1½" × 42" (84 total)

From the White, cut:
12 strips, 7½" × 42"
112 strips, 1" × 42"

From the Shadow, cut:
11 strips, 7½" × 42"
10 strips, 2½" × 42"

TRY STARCH

Starching your fabric before cutting helps to keep it manageable when cutting and sewing narrow strips.

MAKING THE PYRAMID UNITS

Using the template plastic and the pattern on page 42, make a pyramid template. Transfer the guideline markings to the template. Press all seam allowances as shown by the arrows in the illustrations.

1 Sew four White 1"-wide strips and three colored 1½"-wide strips together alternately. Sew a matching 1¾"-wide strip to the top of the panel and another to the bottom to make an 8"-wide striped panel. Press. Make two panels in each of the 14 solids.

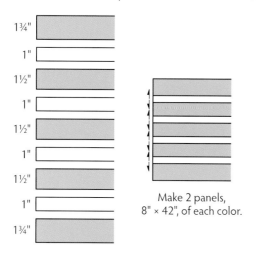

Make 2 panels,
8" × 42", of each color.

2 Place the pyramid template on a striped panel, matching the guideline on the template with the bottom seam of the panel. Cut one pyramid.

3 Rotate the template 180°, matching the guideline with the top seam of the panel and matching the template edge to the previously cut edge. Cut a second pyramid.

4 Continue in this manner to cut a total of 174 pyramids.

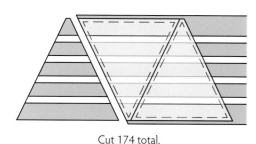

Cut 174 total.

5 In the same manner, cut 90 White pyramids and 84 Shadow pyramids from the 7½"-wide strips as shown.

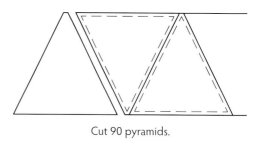

Cut 90 pyramids.

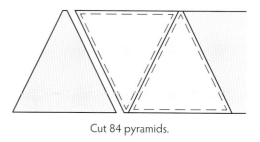

Cut 84 pyramids.

ASSEMBLING THE QUILT TOP

1 Referring to the quilt assembly diagram on page 41, lay out 14 striped pyramids, eight White pyramids, and seven Shadow pyramids. Join the pyramids to make one row A. Repeat to make six rows. Press the seam allowances toward the White and Shadow pyramids.

2 Lay out 15 striped pyramids, seven White pyramids, and seven Shadow pyramids. Join the pyramids to make one row B. Repeat to make six rows. Press the seam allowances toward the White and Shadow pyramids.

3 Sew the rows together, alternating rows A and B. Press the seam allowances in one direction.

4 Trim the side edges, slicing the end pyramids in half, to make a 98½" × 84½" quilt top.

EASY TRIMMING

To trim the sides, place the ¼" line of a ruler on the intersecting points of the A and B rows. Trim, leaving a ¼" seam allowance.

FINISHING THE QUILT

For details on the following steps, download free information at ShopMartingale.com/HowtoQuilt.

1 Cut the backing fabric into three 2⅝-yard lengths. Sew the pieces together side by side.

2 Layer and baste the backing, batting, and quilt top. Quilt as desired. The quilt shown is quilted with straight horizontal lines through the colored stripes.

3 Use the Shadow 2½"-wide strips to make double-fold binding, and then attach the binding to the quilt.

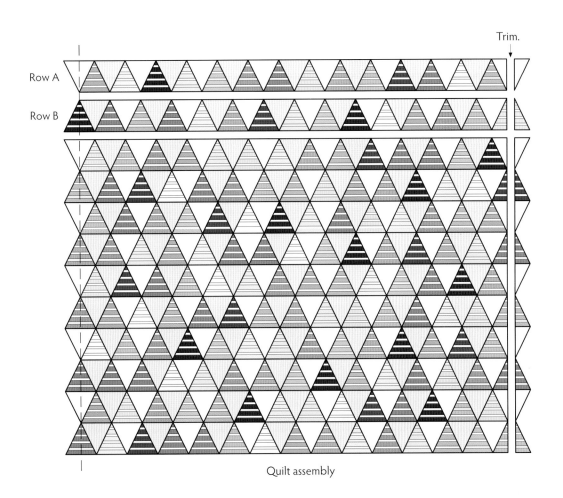

Row A

Row B

Trim.

Quilt assembly

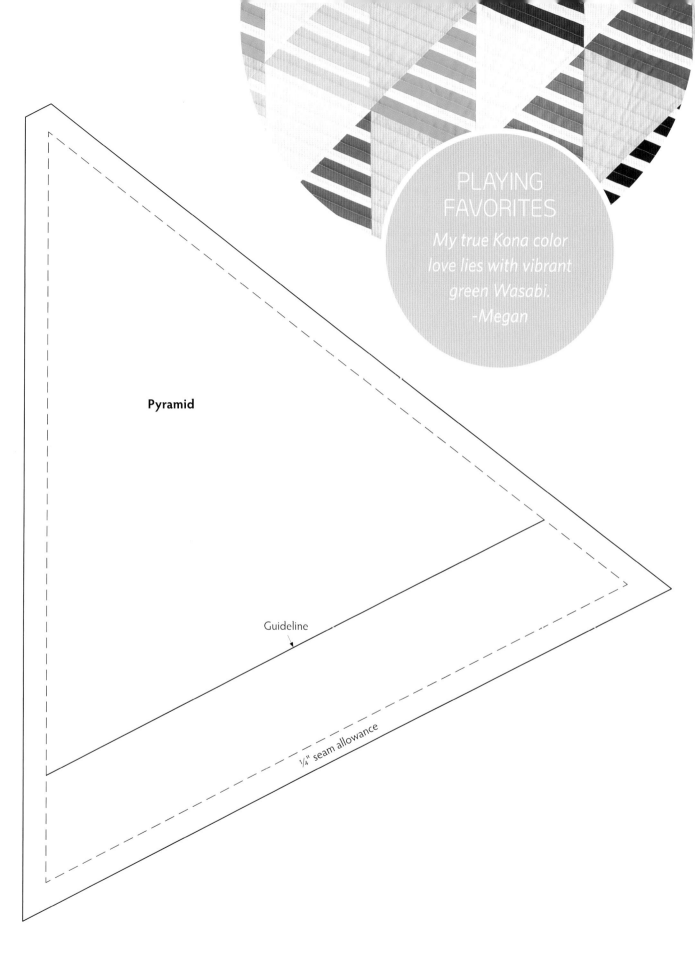

Pyramid

Guideline

¼" seam allowance

TRIBAL BEAT

Designed and pieced by Angela Walters

Art Deco is often characterized as featuring bold geometric shapes, clear and precise lines, and rich colors. This original design fits that description, though at the same time it could certainly be called modern.

FINISHED QUILT: 84½" × 105½" • FINISHED BLOCK: 14" × 23"

MATERIALS

Yardage is based on 42"-wide Kona Cotton solids.

4 yards of Prussian for blocks

4¾ yards of Pool for blocks

2½ yards of Ash for blocks and binding

1¾ yards of Aloe for blocks

7⅞ yards of fabric for backing

93" × 114" piece of batting

CUTTING

All measurements include ¼"-wide seam allowances.

From the Prussian, cut:

3 strips, 8" x 42"; crosscut into 12 squares, 8" × 8"

3 strips, 14½" x 42"; crosscut into:
  6 rectangles, 7½" × 14½"
  6 rectangles, 6½" × 14½"

5 strips, 2½" x 42"; crosscut into:
  18 rectangles, 2½" × 4½"
  36 squares, 2½" × 2½"

3 strips, 16½" x 42"; crosscut into 72 strips,
  1½" × 16½"

From the Pool, cut:

5 strips, 8" x 42"; crosscut into 24 squares, 8" × 8"

3 strips, 16½" x 42"; crosscut into:
  24 strips, 2½" × 16½"
  24 strips, 1½" × 16½"

2 strips, 14½" x 42"; crosscut into 24 strips,
  2½" × 14½"

1 strip, 12½" x 42"; crosscut into 12 strips,
  2½" × 12½"

4 strips, 2½" x 42"; crosscut into:
  6 rectangles, 2½" × 4½"
  12 squares, 2½" × 2½"

From the Ash, cut:

2 strips, 8" x 42"; crosscut into 6 squares, 8" × 8"

10 strips, 2½" × 42"

1 strip, 16½" x 42"; crosscut into 12 strips, 2½" × 16½"

1 strip, 14½" x 42"; crosscut into 12 strips, 2½" × 14½"

1 strip, 12½" x 42"; crosscut into 6 strips, 2½" × 12½"

From the Aloe, cut:

2 strips, 8" x 42"; crosscut into 6 squares, 8" × 8"

1 strip, 16½" x 42"; crosscut into 12 strips, 2½" × 16½"

1 strip, 14½" x 42"; crosscut into 12 strips, 2½" × 14½"

1 strip, 12½" x 42"; crosscut into 6 strips, 2½" × 12½"

MAKING THE BLOCKS

Press all seam allowances as shown by the arrows in the illustrations.

1 Sew a Prussian 2½" square to one end of a Pool 2½" × 14½" strip. Press the seam allowances toward the square. Make two. Sew a Prussian 2½" × 4½" rectangle to one end of a Pool 2½" × 12½" strip. Press the seam allowances toward the Prussian strip.

Make 2.   Make 1.

2 Sew the pieced strips, two Pool 2½" × 16½" strips, and four Prussian 1½" × 16½" strips together in the order shown to make a 14½" × 16½" pieced rectangle. Press. Repeat to make 12 units. In the same manner, make six Ash/Prussian pieced rectangles and six Aloe/Pool pieced rectangles.

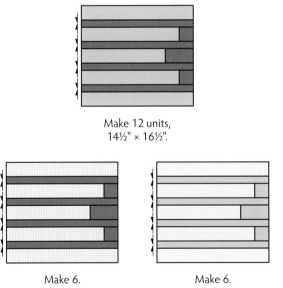

Make 12 units,
14½" × 16½".

Make 6.   Make 6.

3 Place a Prussian 8" square and a Pool 8" square right sides together. Draw a diagonal line from corner to corner on the wrong side of the top square. Sew ¼" away from both sides of the drawn line. Cut on the drawn line to make two half-square-triangle units. Press. Trim the units to measure 7½" square. Make 24.

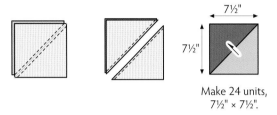

Make 24 units,
7½" × 7½".

4 In the same manner, make 12 Ash/Pool and 12 Aloe/Pool half-square-triangle units.

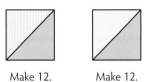

Make 12.   Make 12.

5 Sew two Prussian/Pool half-square-triangle units together as shown to make a 7½" × 14½" flying-geese unit. Press. Make 12. In the same manner, make six Ash/Pool flying-geese units and six Aloe/Pool flying-geese units.

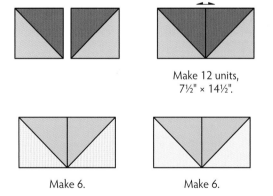

Make 12 units,
7½" × 14½".

Make 6.   Make 6.

6 Sew a Prussian/Pool flying-geese unit to a Prussian/Pool pieced rectangle to make a block that measures 14½" × 23½". Make 12. Press.

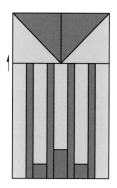

Make 12 blocks,
14½" × 23½".

7 In the same manner, make six blocks using the Ash/Prussian pieced rectangles and Ash/Pool flying-geese units. Make six blocks using the Aloe/Pool pieced rectangles and Aloe/Pool flying-geese units.

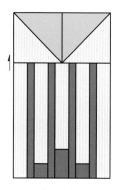

Make 6 blocks,
14½" × 23½".

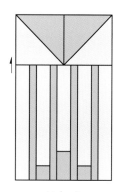

Make 6.

ASSEMBLING THE QUILT ROWS

Lay out one Prussian 7½" × 14½" rectangle, one Prussian 6½" × 14½" rectangle, two Prussian/Pool blocks, one Aloe/Pool block, and one Ash/Prussian block in a vertical row. Sew the units together in the row. Press to make a 14½" × 105½" block row. Make six.

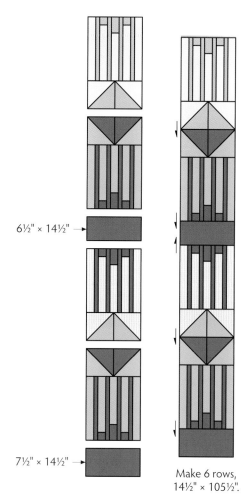

6½" × 14½" →

7½" × 14½" →

Make 6 rows,
14½" × 105½".

PICKING A PALETTE

Blue, green, and gray make for a soothing array of colors. For an entirely different feel, make this quilt in red, orange, and yellow.

ASSEMBLING THE QUILT TOP

1 Lay out the block rows, rotating every other row 180°.

2 Sew the block rows together to make an 84½" × 105½" quilt top. Press.

FINISHING THE QUILT

For details on the following steps, download free information at ShopMartingale.com/HowtoQuilt.

1 Cut the backing fabric into three 2⅝-yard lengths. Sew the pieces together side by side.

2 Layer and baste the backing, batting, and quilt top. Quilt as desired. The quilt shown is machine quilted with straight lines outlining the rectangles and with lines radiating from the points of the triangles.

3 Use the Ash 2½"-wide strips to make double-fold binding, and then attach the binding to the quilt.

Quilt assembly

COLUMBIA

Designed and pieced by Debbie Grifka

Architecture—from the bold shapes of modern buildings to the beautiful detail of older structures, there is always something to notice and admire. The inspiration for Columbia came from a detail on a building's pillars at Columbia University. This quilt is different from those pillars, but that's the fun of inspiration—take it and run with it!

FINISHED QUILT: 60½" × 80½"

MATERIALS

Yardage is based on 42"-wide Kona Cotton solids.

3½ yards of Nautical

2½ yards of White

5¼ yards of fabric for backing

69" × 89" piece of batting

CUTTING

All measurements include ¼"-wide seam allowances.

From the Nautical, cut on the *lengthwise* grain:
1 strip, 24½" × 81"; crosscut into:
    1 rectangle, 22½" × 24½"
    1 rectangle, 21½" × 24½"
    2 rectangles, 10½" × 24½"
    1 strip, 4½" × 24½"
    1 strip, 3½" × 24½"
2 strips, 4½" × 80½" (C and E)
2 strips, 2½" × 80½" (A and G)

From the remaining Nautical, cut on the *crosswise* grain:
14 strips, 2½" × 42". Reserve 8 strips for binding
    and then crosscut the remaining 6 strips into:
    1 strip, 2½" × 21½"
    6 strips, 2½" × 10½"
    21 rectangles, 2½" × 4½"
    3 rectangles, 2½" × 3½"

From the White, cut on the *lengthwise* grain:
1 strip, 8½" × 80½" (J)
1 strip, 2½" × 80½" (H)
1 strip, 10½" × 81"; crosscut into:
    1 rectangle, 10½" × 16½"
    1 rectangle, 10½" × 15½"
    3 squares, 10½" × 10½"
    1 strip, 4½" × 10½"
    1 strip, 3½" × 10½"
2 strips, 2½" × 75"; crosscut into 5 strips,
    2½" × 24½"
1 strip, 2½" × 60"; crosscut into 23 squares,
    2½" × 2½"

ASSEMBLING THE VERTICAL COLUMNS

1 Referring to the quilt assembly diagram on page 51, sew 10 White 2½" squares and nine Nautical 2½" × 4½" strips together, alternating them. Sew one Nautical 2½" × 3½" rectangle to the left of the strip and the Nautical 2½" × 21½" strip to the right. Press the seam allowances toward the Nautical pieces. The strip should measure 80½" long. Label it row B.

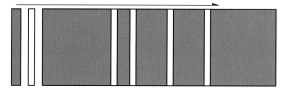

Row B,
2½" × 80½".

2 Sew one Nautical 3½" × 24½" strip, one Nautical 22½" × 24½" rectangle, one Nautical 4½" × 24½" strip, two Nautical 10½" × 24½" rectangles, and one Nautical 21½" × 24½" rectangle together alternately with five White 2½" × 24½" strips as shown. Press the seam allowances toward the Nautical pieces. The strip should measure 80½" long. Label it row D.

Row D,
24½" × 80½".

3 Sew 13 White 2½" squares and 12 Nautical 2½" × 4½" strips together alternately. Sew the remaining Nautical 2½" × 3½" rectangles to the ends of the strip. Press the seam allowances toward the Nautical pieces. The strip should measure 80½" long. Label it row F.

Row F,
2½" × 80½".

4 Sew one White 10½" × 15½" rectangle, three White 10½" squares, one White 10½" × 16½" rectangle, one White 4½" × 10½" strip, and one White 3½" × 10½" strip together alternately with six Nautical 2½" × 10½" strips as shown. Press the seam allowances toward the Nautical pieces. The strip should measure 80½" long. Label it row I.

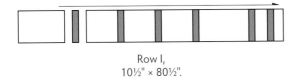

Row I,
10½" × 80½".

CAN'T GO WRONG!

With these fabrics, there's no right side or wrong side—one of the great things about using solids!

ASSEMBLING THE QUILT TOP

1 Lay out the pieced rows and strips A, C, E, G, H, and J in alphabetical order.

2 Sew the rows and strips together. Press the seam allowances toward the strips to make a 60½" × 80½" quilt top.

FINISHING THE QUILT

For details on the following steps, download free information at ShopMartingale.com/HowtoQuilt.

1 Cut the backing fabric into two 2⅝-yard lengths. Sew the pieces together side by side.

2 Layer and baste the backing, batting, and quilt top. Quilt as desired. The quilt shown is machine quilted with parallel horizontal lines.

3 Use the remaining Nautical 2½"-wide strips to make double-fold binding, and then attach the binding to the quilt.

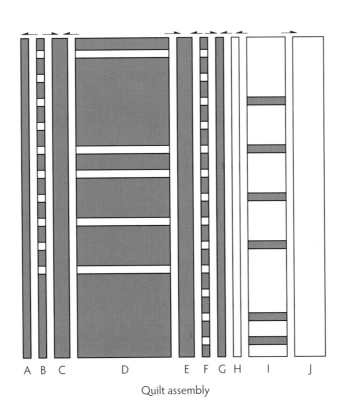

A B C   D   E F G H   I   J

Quilt assembly

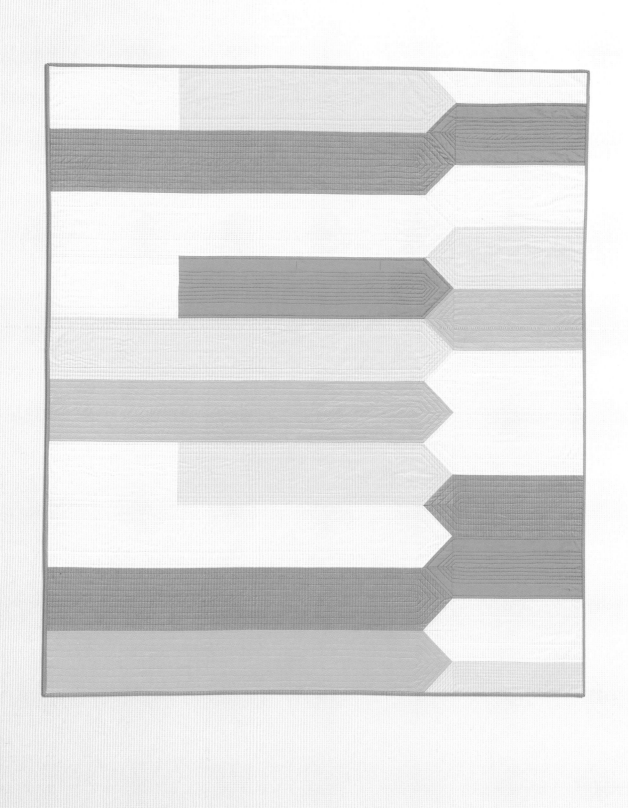

INTERSECTION

Designed and pieced by Nydia Kehnle

Combine cool and vibrant green hues with soft shades of gray to make a striking asymmetrical design. The quilt top comes together quickly from two easy-to-piece panels.

FINISHED QUILT: 54" × 60½"

MATERIALS

Yardage is based on 42"-wide Kona Cotton solids.

1½ yards of Oyster for piecing

¾ yard of Pool for piecing

1 yard of Smoke for piecing and binding

½ yard of Jade Green for piecing

⅞ yard of Wasabi for piecing

3⅔ yards of fabric for backing

60" × 66" piece of batting

CUTTING

All measurements include ¼"-wide seam allowances.

From the Oyster, cut:
2 strips, 6½" × 41"
4 strips, 6½" × 42"; crosscut into 7 strips, 6½" × 13½"
1 strip, 3½" × 42"; crosscut into 9 squares, 3½" × 3½"
1 strip, 3½" × 13½"

From the Pool, cut:
2 strips, 6½" × 41"
1 strip, 6½" × 13½"
2 squares, 3½" × 3½"

From the Jade Green, cut:
1 strip, 6½" × 28"
2 strips, 6½" × 13½"
4 squares, 3½" × 3½"

From the Wasabi, cut:
1 strip, 6½" × 41"
2 strips, 6½" × 28"
1 strip, 6½" × 13½"
1 strip, 3½" × 13½"
3 squares, 3½" × 3½"

From Smoke, cut:
2 strips, 6½" × 41"
1 strip, 6½" × 13½"
2 squares, 3½" × 3½"
6 strips, 2½" × 42"

ASSEMBLING THE PIECED SECTIONS

Press all seam allowances as shown by the arrows in the illustrations. The quilt contains two pieced sections: A and B. Refer to the layout diagram for the position of the numbered pieces in each section. Make sure to keep the pieces organized in order to connect the triangles in section A to the matching strips in section B.

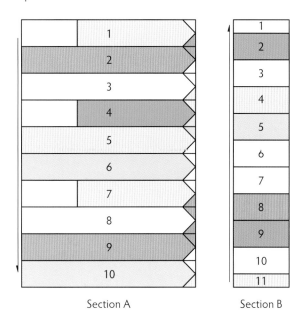

Section A   Section B

1 To make rows A1 and A7, sew an Oyster 6½" × 13½" strip to one end of each Wasabi 6½" × 28" strip. Press. For row A4, sew one Oyster 6½" × 13½" strip to one end of the Jade Green 6½" × 28" strip and press. The three pieced strips should measure 6½" × 41". Rows 2, 3, 5, 6, 8, 9, and 10 are all 6½" × 41" strips.

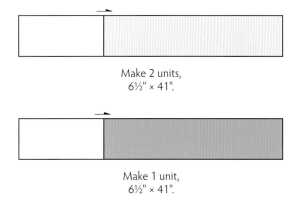

Make 2 units,
6½" × 41".

Make 1 unit,
6½" × 41".

2 Draw a diagonal line from corner to corner on the wrong side of each 3½" square. Place one marked Oyster square on the top-right corner of row A1, orienting the line as shown. Sew on the line. Trim the fabric, leaving a ¼" seam allowance, and press. Repeat to sew a Jade Green square to the bottom-right corner in the same manner.

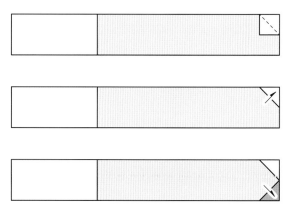

3 Repeat the process in step 2 to sew squares to the top- and bottom-right corners of rows A2 through A10, referring to the layout diagram at left for the color placement for each row. Join the rows along the long edges; press. The section should measure 41" × 60½".

4 For section B, lay out all of the 13½"-long strips, referring to the layout diagram at left for placement. Note that B1 and B11 are the 3½"-wide strips and B2–B10 are the 6½"-wide strips. Join the strips; press. The section should measure 13½" × 60½".

PICKING A PALETTE

Nydia wanted a color palette that worked well in a home, and she loves to combine neutrals with punchy bright colors. She chose Wasabi to be the standalone hue, so she paired a couple neutrals (Oyster and Smoke) with green-blues (Jade Green and Pool).

ASSEMBLING THE QUILT TOP

Referring to the quilt assembly diagram below, place sections A and B right sides together, carefully matching the seamlines so that the triangles along the seam appear connected to the adjoining strips; pin. Sew the sections together and press. The quilt top should measure 54" × 60½".

FINISHING THE QUILT

For details on the following steps, download free information at ShopMartingale.com/HowtoQuilt.

1 Cut the backing fabric into two 65" lengths. Sew the pieces together side by side.

2 Layer and baste the backing, batting, and quilt top. Quilt as desired. The quilt shown is machine quilted by echoing the color bars and points.

3 Use the Smoke 2½"-wide strips to make double-fold binding, and then attach the binding to the quilt.

PLAYING FAVORITES

Wasabi works as a yellow and as a green, and it pairs well with so many different colors.
-Nydia

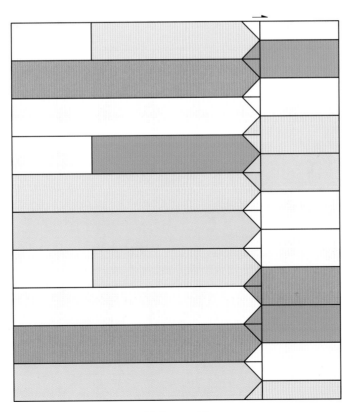

Quilt assembly

8-BIT

Designed and pieced by Janice Zeller Ryan

There's so much to like about this fascinating design—the colors, the stripes, the layout, the shading. The carefully planned color placement creates movement and visual impact.

FINISHED QUILT: 84½" × 108½" • FINISHED BLOCK: 12" × 12"

MATERIALS

Yardage is based on 42"-wide Kona Cotton solids.

5 yards of White OR 3 packs of Kona Skinny Strips for blocks

2½ yards of Black OR 1 pack of Kona Skinny Strips for blocks and binding

1¾ yards of Sage for blocks

½ yard of Coral for blocks

⅜ yard of Baby Pink for blocks

⅝ yard of Yarrow for blocks

⅝ yard of Pomegranate for blocks

1 yard of Sky for blocks

1 yard of Shadow for blocks

⅜ yard of Light Parfait for blocks

¼ yard of Butter for blocks

8 yards of fabric for backing

93" × 117" piece of batting

CUTTING

All measurements include ¼"-wide seam allowances.

From the White, cut:
117 strips, 1½" × 42"

From the Black, cut:
10 strips, 2½" × 42"
38 strips, 1½" × 42"

From the Sage, cut:
1 strip, 2½" × 42"; crosscut into
    4 squares, 2½" × 2½"
2 strips, 4½" × 42"; crosscut into
    16 squares, 4½" × 4½"
29 strips, 1½" × 42"

From the Coral, cut:
1 strip, 2½" × 42"; crosscut into
    5 squares, 2½" × 2½"
2 strips, 4½" × 42"; crosscut into
    16 squares, 4½" × 4½"

From the Baby Pink, cut:
2 strips, 4½" × 42"; crosscut into
    16 squares, 4½" × 4½"

From the Yarrow, cut:
1 strip, 2½" × 42"; crosscut into
    4 squares, 2½" × 2½"
3 strips, 4½" × 42"; crosscut into
    20 squares, 4½" × 4½"

From the Pomegranate, cut:
4 strips, 2½" × 42"; crosscut into
    50 squares, 2½" × 2½"
2 strips, 4½" × 42"; crosscut into
    16 squares, 4½" × 4½"

From the Sky, cut:
2 strips, 4½" × 42"; crosscut into
    16 squares, 4½" × 4½"
15 strips, 1½" × 42"

From the Shadow, cut:
20 strips, 1½" × 42"

From the Light Parfait, cut:
2 strips, 4½" × 42"; crosscut into
    16 squares, 4½" × 4½"

From the Butter, cut:
1 strip, 4½" × 42"; crosscut into
    8 squares, 4½" × 4½"

MAKING THE BLOCKS

This quilt is made from alternating Nine Patch and Courthouse Steps blocks. You will trim the 1½" strips as you sew. All seam allowances should be pressed toward the darker fabric so that they don't show through the white fabric in the finished quilt.

Making the Nine Patch Blocks

1 To make a Nine Patch center, sew Black 1½"-wide strips to the top and bottom of a Yarrow 2½" square. Trim the Black strips even with the edges of the square. Then sew Black 1½"-wide strips to both sides of the Yarrow square. Trim the unit to 4½" square. Repeat to make four Black/Yarrow units.

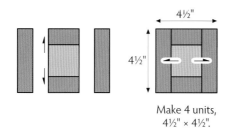

4½"

4½"

Make 4 units,
4½" × 4½".

PLAYING FAVORITES

I love the variety of Kona colors available and the bold visual statement they make in a quilt.
-Janice

CHAIN SEWING THE BLOCK CENTERS

Rather than cut all of the pieces needed for each block to a specific length first, you'll be starting with long strips, which means you can chain sew the blocks. This makes for speedier construction.

For step 1 at left, arrange the Yarrow squares on top of one Black strip. Sew all of the squares to the same strip and press the seam allowances toward the black strip. Then, cut the units apart with your rotary cutter and ruler. In the same manner, sew the Yarrow/ Black units to another Black strip so that you have a Black segment on each side of the Yarrow square. Repeat for the two remaining sides of the Yarrow squares.

You can use this method for step 2 as well, making all of the block centers in this assembly-line fashion.

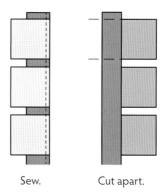

Sew.   Cut apart.

2 Repeat step 1 to make the number of center units in each color combination as indicated.

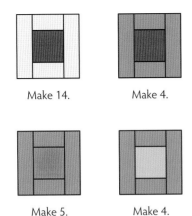

Make 14.   Make 4.

Make 5.   Make 4.

3 Sew two Black and two White 1½"-wide strips together, alternating them. Press the seam allowances toward the Black strips and lightly starch, if desired. Make four Black/White strip sets, five Sage/White strip sets, four Shadow/White strip sets, and three Sky/White strip sets.

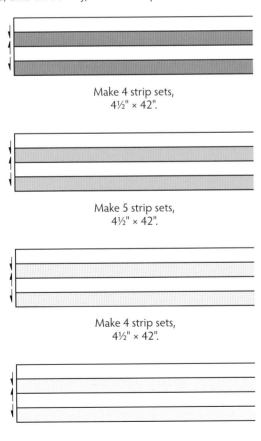

Make 4 strip sets,
4½" × 42".

Make 5 strip sets,
4½" × 42".

Make 4 strip sets,
4½" × 42".

Make 3 strip sets,
4½" × 42".

STRIP-SET SAVVY

- *When sewing strip sets, use a shorter stitch (about a 2.0 setting on your machine) to prevent cut seams from unraveling.*

- *Use a walking foot and be careful not to stretch the strips as you sew.*

- *Trim the end of the strip set to a 90° angle after cutting every two or three segments.*

4 Cut the required number of 4½"-wide segments from strip sets as indicated.

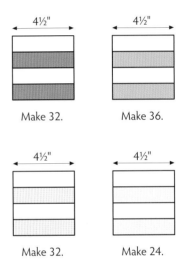

4½"   4½"

Make 32.   Make 36.

4½"   4½"

Make 32.   Make 24.

5 Lay out four Black/White segments, four Sage 4½" squares, and one Yarrow/Black center unit. Join the units into rows. Sew the rows together to complete a Nine Patch block that measures 12½" square. Press. Make four.

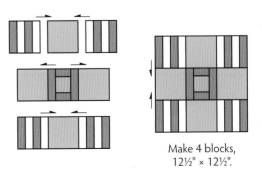

Make 4 blocks,
12½" × 12½".

6 Repeat step 5 to make the required number of Nine Patch blocks in each colorway as indicated.

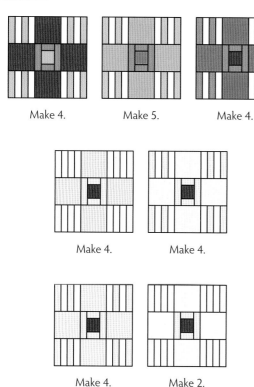

Make 4.   Make 5.   Make 4.

Make 4.   Make 4.

Make 4.   Make 2.

Making the Courthouse Steps Blocks

Chain sew the Courthouse Steps blocks in the same manner as the Nine Patch block centers. Press each seam allowance toward the last strip added.

1 Sew White strips to the sides of a Pomegranate 2½" square. Trim the White strips even with the edges of the square. Sew White strips to the top and bottom of the square. Trim the unit to 4½" square. Make 32 center units.

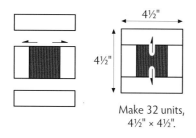

4½"

4½"

Make 32 units,
4½" × 4½".

2 Repeat to sew Sage, Black, and White strips to a center unit as shown, adding four rounds of strips to the center unit. Sew the top and bottom strips to the center unit first. Press and trim, and then sew the side strips. Repeat to make a 12½" square block. Make 18 Sage, Black, and White blocks.

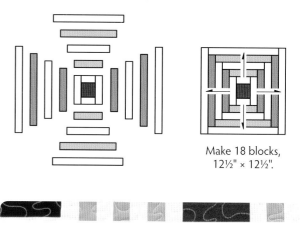

Make 18 blocks,
12½" × 12½".

MAKE A TEST BLOCK

Make one complete block and measure to make sure it's 12½" square. If it's not the right size, adjust your seam allowances for the remaining blocks accordingly.

3 Repeat step 2 to make the number of blocks in each colorway as indicated.

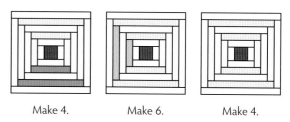

Make 4.   Make 6.   Make 4.

ASSEMBLING THE QUILT TOP

1 Arrange the blocks on a design wall or the floor, alternating the Courthouse Steps and Nine Patch blocks as shown in the quilt assembly diagram below, to make nine rows of seven blocks each.

2 Sew the blocks into rows. Press.

3 Sew the rows together to complete an 84½" × 108½" quilt top.

FINISHING THE QUILT

For details on the following steps, download free information at ShopMartingale.com/HowtoQuilt.

1 Cut the backing fabric into three 2⅔-yard lengths. Sew the pieces together side by side.

2 Layer and baste the backing, batting, and quilt top. Quilt as desired. The quilt shown is machine quilted in an allover meandering pattern.

3 Use the Black 2½"-wide strips to make double-fold binding, and then attach the binding to the quilt.

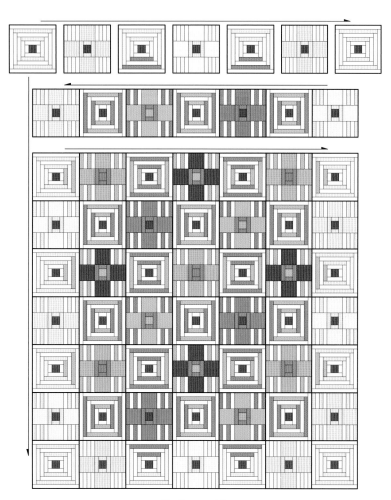

Quilt assembly

COLOR PALETTES

SPECTRUM *page 7*

● Yarrow ● Grellow ● Canary
Banana ● Meringue ● Peridot
● Bonsai ● Peapod ● Limelight
● Wasabi ● Celestial ● Caribbean
● Jade Green ● Candy Green ● Capri
● Bright Periwinkle ● Heliotrope
● Morning Glory ● Violet ● Pansy
● Berry ● Dark Violet ● Geranium
● Gumdrop ● Blush Pink ● Cerise
● Valentine ● Honeysuckle ● Camellia
● Bubble Gum

RAGGED EDGES *page 11*

● Iron ● Titanium ○ White
● Graphite ● Silver ● Pepper

LANTERNS *page 13*

● Lime ● Sprout ● Peapod ● Cactus
● Zucchini ● Artichoke ● Curry
● Corn Yellow ● Sunflower ● Buttercup
● Canary ● Citrus ● Cheddar
● Papaya ● School Bus ● Orange
● Mango ● Carrot ● Tangerine
● Flame ● Coral ● Lipstick ● Tomato
● Poppy ● Red ● Pomegranate ● Ruby
● Rich Red ● Coal

GANDER *page 19*

● Flame ● Kumquat ● Natural
● Aqua ● Azure

62

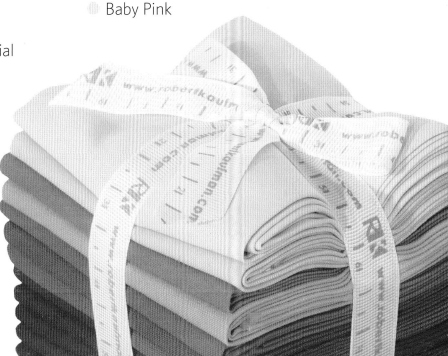

MEET THE CONTRIBUTORS

ELIZABETH DACKSON
DontCallMeBetsy.com

DEBBIE GRIFKA
EschHouseQuilts.com

CORTNEY HEIMERL
CortneyHeimerl.com

SHEA HENDERSON
EmptyBobbinSewing.com

JULIE HERMAN
JayBirdQuilts.com

HEATHER JONES
HeatherJonesStudio.com

NYDIA KEHNLE
NydiaKehnle.com

MEGAN PITZ
CanoeRidgeCreations.com

JANICE ZELLER RYAN
BetterOffThread.com

KRISTI SCHROEDER
InitialKStudio.com

ANITA GROSSMAN SOLOMON
MakeItSimpler.com

ANGELA WALTERS
QuiltingIsMyTherapy.com

CHRISTA WATSON
ChristaQuilts.com

What's your creative passion?

Find it at **ShopMartingale.com**

books • eBooks • ePatterns • blog • free projects
videos • tutorials • inspiration • giveaways